A Little Further

A Guide for Navigating Garden Seasons

Sandra R. Bitten

Copyright © 2023 by Sandra R. Bitten

A Little Further: A Guide for Navigating Garden Seasons
by Sandra R. Bitten

Printed in the United States of America

ISBN 979-8-218-96778-9

Unless otherwise specified, Scripture quotations are taken from the New King James Version®. Copyright © 1982 by Thomas Nelson. Used by permission. All rights reserved.

Scripture quotations marked ESV are taken from The Holy Bible, English Standard Version. ESV® Text Edition: 2016. Copyright © 2001 by Crossway Bibles, a publishing ministry of Good News Publishers. All rights reserved.

Scripture quotations marked NIV are taken from The Holy Bible, New International Version®, NIV® Copyright ©1973, 1978, 1984, 2011 by Biblica, Inc.® Used by permission. All rights reserved worldwide.

Scripture quotations marked NLT are taken from *The Holy Bible*, New Living Translation, copyright © 1996, 2004, 2015 by Tyndale House Foundation. Used by permission of Tyndale House Publishers, Inc., Carol Stream, Illinois 60188. All rights reserved.

Scripture quotations marked TPT are from The Passion Translation®. Copyright © 2017, 2018, 2020 by Passion & Fire Ministries, Inc. Used by permission. All rights reserved. ThePassionTranslation.com.

All rights reserved by the author. The author guarantees all contents are original and do not infringe upon the legal rights of any other person or work. No part of this book may be reproduced, distributed, or transmitted in any form or by any means without prior written permission of the publisher, except in the case of brief quotations for noncommercial use as permitted by copyright law. For permission requests and inquiries, email srbitten@live.com.

PEACE, BE STILL
Acknowledging the Garden

36 Now when they had left the multitude, they took Him along in the boat as He was. And other little boats were also with Him. 37 And a great windstorm arose, and the waves beat into the boat, so that it was already filling. 38 But He was in the stern, asleep on a pillow. And they awoke Him and said to Him, "Teacher, do You not care that we are perishing?"

Mark 4:36-38

You have been there. There is a good chance that you are in such a place at this very second. I am certain you know enough Bible to brush off the disciples' anxiety. You are well aware that, "Peace, be still," is coming to their rescue. *But what about mine?* It is natural to wonder when peace will arrive to still *your* storm.

It feels like serenity is indefinitely pending. *Where is Jesus? Why isn't my Savior saving me? Isn't prayer supposed to change things?* The questions continue surging up in your soul. Everything within you screams, "Run!" The problem is that running resolves nothing. You also aren't quite sure how to escape this wilderness. This furnace of affliction. This pain. Let me share a little secret with you: This place is not meant for escaping.

This place - as uncomfortable and weighty as it is - is divinely designed for such a time as this. There it is! I see you shaking your head! Bless your little baby heart. Fix your face and lean in. This is a hard truth for your heart to accept, I know. Nevertheless, it is a truth with which you must grapple... and ultimately trust. Even your current place of affliction will work together for your good if you trust God to be God.

You want to shout in objection to the unfairness of it all. And that is okay. Shout, cry, and even stomp your feet if needed. You are free to feel every ounce of pain and frustration surging through your body. However, I implore you to resist the urge to stay there. Remember, you signed up for this. When? When you believed in your heart that Jesus is Lord and confessed Him as your Savior, you also agreed to tough times like the one you are currently experiencing.

12 Dear friends, do not be surprised at the fiery ordeal that has come on you to test you, as though something strange were happening to you. 13 But rejoice in as much as you participate in the sufferings of Christ, so that you may be overjoyed when his glory is revealed.

1 Peter 4:12-13, NIV

You do not want to be here but you need to be here. The Lord wants you right where you are, here in the garden. You were drawn to this guide because of the garden. The heaviness you feel is indicative of this appointed place. Your very own Gethsemane. Your crushing place. Don't worry, though. The Lord is with you, and so am I.

Together, we will sit in this place, process this place, and embrace this place. The oil of the anointing will flow when you willingly go a little further into the garden. You can do it! I am sure of it! I am here to coach you through the journey. Each week's reading is followed by three questions and a challenge to *go a little further*. Take your time. Read the devotional passage as many times as needed for the truths to sink in. Really sit in the questions. Meditate on them and respond honestly. This isn't a race; it is designed to be a place of healing and discovery. I trust you will find that answering one question per day is a beautiful pace.

    You are unsure if you are ready, I know. It's okay. Take my hand. Let's walk a little further into the garden together. Slowly.

THE DANGER ZONE
Week One

Hope deferred makes the heart sick, but a dream fulfilled is a tree of life.
Proverbs 13:12, NLT

There is **nothing** more dangerous than a disappointed Christian. I have been walking with the Lord for a long time, and I know plenty of people with a distorted view of how life in Christ should be. The expectation is often a carefree existence of ease and fulfilled promises without problems or stress and not one setback in sight. That is simply not true! Neither is it realistic.

During those early days of being new to the faith, everything is *happy, happy, joy, joy*! We are on fire for God and ready to obey His every command. How exciting those times are! Then, life happens and it continues happening. Sometimes the waves of hardship are widespread. We handle that better. Anyone who has experienced adversity knows it is a little easier to catch your breath when the next hit doesn't come directly on the heels of the one before it. Unfortunately, there are seasons when challenges roll in as one unrelenting sucker punch after another. That is when the rubber really meets the road. Will our faith waver? We find ourselves wondering...

Where is God? What is the point? When will this end?

The longer we walk with Christ - the more we fervently follow after Jesus with our whole hearts - the more we begin to see that it is actually easier not to do so. Yes, you read correctly. Those who go with the world's flow and conform to the ways of culture do not find themselves dodging an adversary's fiery darts. Why would they? They pose no threat to him! They accept the world's way of behaving and believing and leave the battles to us Blood-bought believers. Being let down in the world's arena means individuals can only be disappointed in themselves or other people, not a higher power. If *we* are the problem, all that is needed is a well-developed plan to fix our shortcomings. In come the self-help books and home-grown ideologies. These avenues of thought lead to a place of self-realization wherein one's identity in Christ with all its inherent power and authority is denied. How many of us truly understand what happens to a branch when it is disconnected from its source?

4 Abide in Me, and I in you. As the branch cannot bear fruit of itself, unless it abides in the vine, neither can you, unless you abide in Me. 5 "I am the vine, you are the branches. He who abides in Me, and I in him, bears much fruit; for without Me you can do nothing.

John 15:4-5

We are living during a time when Christians find it easy and vastly acceptable to blend in. To hide in the shadows of carnality. To keep our distance from righteousness. But things are living in those far-off places of compromise that keep the power of God from working in our lives. Ephesians 2 speaks of our enemy, the prince of the power of the air, who casts lies and would consume our lives with the lusts and desires of the flesh *if* we allow him. Satan's whole intent and self-appointed purpose is to keep believers from believing! He wants us to become the antithesis of who God called us to be. His attacks are designed to make us lose hope in the Lord's faithfulness when we are faced with odds that seem insurmountable.

The enemy intends for you to grow weary in the garden. In the hard thing. The enemy has his intention; yet, you have a choice: yield to the danger of disappointment or trust that the garden will ultimately produce good. Only you can decide for *you*.

DAY ONE

Describe the conflict you are currently experiencing. How is this season or situation threatening to disconnect you from Christ?

_____
_____
_____
_____
_____
_____
_____
_____
_____
_____
_____
_____
_____
_____
_____
_____
_____
_____
_____
_____
_____
_____
_____
_____

DAY TWO

Think about what makes this place of conflict so uncomfortable. Consider all that you are feeling. Although it may be uncomfortable, honor your heart by allowing yourself to feel and identify each emotion.

Now, what hard thing is God calling you to do despite the discomfort?

DAY THREE

When did things change? Take a few minutes to reflect on the shift from zeal to the place of disappointment, fear, and/or any other heavy emotions you are currently navigating.

_____
_____
_____
_____
_____
_____
_____
_____
_____
_____
_____
_____
_____
_____
_____
_____
_____
_____
_____
_____
_____
_____
_____

GO A LITTLE FURTHER...

Record 3 promises the Lord has given you. How does your current conflict shake your faith in these promises? Which passages of scripture will you stand on to persevere *through* the conflict and contend for your promises?

THE GOOD LIFE
Week Two

A thief has only one thing in mind—he wants to steal, slaughter, and destroy. But I have come to give you everything in abundance, more than you expect —life in its fullness until you overflow!

John 10:10, TPT

All the promises of God to His children are yes and amen in Christ (2 Corinthians 1:20). According to Psalm 84:11, there is no good thing that the Lord withholds from those who walk uprightly. Not one! Does that mean life will be sunshine and rainbows all the time? No. What I can promise you (because the Word assures me) is that God has called us to a realm in the Spirit where a life of abundance, overflow, and impactfulness is not only attainable but expected. The standard is for us to triumph over our enemies. We use that term loosely, so allow me to further define it. Our real enemy is separation from God. Apart from Him, we cannot live out our purpose or exercise the spiritual gifts awarded to every believer.

As followers of Christ, our lives are meant to effect change in the world. The offer of overflow is not for us to build selfish kingdoms unto ourselves but to advance God's Kingdom. Light is designed to spread, to push back against the darkness. Take a look around. Darkness is vast and heavy.

We do not just see it; we also feel the weight of it. To the untrained eye, the darkness is winning. Can I submit to you today that the Kingdom is not out of weapons in this fight against the enemy of violence and murder that is sweeping over this nation? Over the world. Each of us has a part to play. God has given us all strategic assignments.

So, why isn't it working? Why aren't *we* working??

Sadly, some of us don't even know what our assignments are. And yet, some of us are fully aware of the unique calls on our lives and remain silent - unmoving and unconcerned about the plight of nations. They are happy just to live a good life. I am not saying a good life is not to be longed for or sought after, but it must come after we seek first the kingdom of God and His righteousness (Matthew 6:33).

From the news to social media to everyday life, it seems as if there is no answer to remedy the madness. How do we intervene? The world is moving at such a rapid rate of change. Technology is constantly upping the ante. Thus, creating new highways and modes of transportation for anger, violence, and messages of hate to freely reign. Lies and twisted truths are empowered to deceive millions by the second. WHAT DO WE DO? How do we stop senseless killings? What can we do to issue a cease and desist to the chaos? Sure, policies can be enacted to wage war on drugs and curb the violence in our streets, but what is to be done now that a full-on attack is being waged on our children from every angle? While we are preoccupied with building good lives, our children are losing their lives, having their innocence stolen, and their sense of safety destroyed.

This is a message for the Church today, a clarion call to every child of God. Dear Christian, you were created to **BE THE**

DIFFERENCE. I am not necessarily speaking to those politically connected who can change laws, but wouldn't that be great? This is bigger than being elected to any government office. This is a hard place. *We* are in a hard place. Each of us believes someone else can help. The truth is we can all help. We should all be working toward the same goal.

A unified front is required and the right weaponry too. There is no excuse to not band together to wage war. We can storm the gates of hell on our knees. During our morning walk. From the pages of our journals. On the drive home from work. As believers, all we must do is activate the weapon of prayer and this weapon will effectively avail (James 5:16). The garden, as uncomfortable and inconvenient as it may be, is for our good because it produces the maturity needed to stand on God's Word. This hard place teaches us to persevere through life's trials by prevailing in prayer.

DAY ONE

Describe how you perceive the intersection between purpose and prayer. What value does this place hold in your life?

DAY TWO

Your faith and prayers strike a mighty blow against the enemy's plans to defeat you! Think about that. You are POWERFUL!

How has God called you to target your prayers? For whom is He instructing to pray?

_____
_____
_____
_____
_____
_____
_____
_____
_____
_____
_____
_____
_____
_____
_____
_____
_____
_____
_____
_____

DAY THREE

What do you need to either get back on the front lines of prayer or to remain steadfast on the frontlines of prayer?

GO A LITTLE FURTHER...

The writer of Hebrews tells us that without faith, it is impossible to please God (Hebrews 11:6). Use the space below to repent of faithlessness that has caused you to pull back from prayer or your purpose in any way.

THE GARDEN PRAYER
Week Three

36 Then Jesus went with them to a place called Gethsemane, and he said to his disciples, "Sit here, while I go over there and pray." 37 And taking with him Peter and the two sons of Zebedee, he began to be sorrowful and troubled. 38 Then he said to them, "My soul is very sorrowful, even to death; remain here, and watch with me." 39 And going a little farther he fell on his face and prayed, saying, "My Father, if it be possible, let this cup pass from me; nevertheless, not as I will, but as you will." 40 And he came to the disciples and found them sleeping. And he said to Peter, "So, could you not watch with me for one hour? 41 Watch and pray that you may not enter into temptation. The spirit indeed is willing, but the flesh is weak." 42 Again, for the second time, he went away and prayed, "My Father, if this cannot pass unless I drink it, your will be done." 43 And again he came and found them sleeping, for their eyes were heavy. 44 So, leaving them again, he went away and prayed for the third time, saying the same words again.

Matthew 26:36-44, ESV

Do I have permission to challenge your perspective of this week's text? So often we label these verses as the lead-up to Judas' betrayal that catapults us into the Easter story. I am not saying this is wrong, but could it be incomplete? While the traditional view is correct, what else do you see? Look closely. This is our blueprint for how to pray in hard times - the kind of hard times that come with the inward struggle of choosing to battle on behalf of others and seeing the fight through to the end.

Here we find Jesus, our Messiah who willingly left His throne to reconcile us back to the Father, as heavyhearted as can be. He is saddened and depressed about the events that will soon transpire. Rightfully so! To be betrayed, beaten, denied, and crucified is a lot for any person - let alone an innocent person - to endure. Yes, Jesus is fully God, but that does not mean we should ever forget He was also 100% man while on earth. His divinity was all in. His humanity wrestled with thoughts of the pain, torture, and momentary separation from the Father that was soon to come. Remember, the spirit is willing but the flesh is weak. "My Father, if at all possible, let this cup pass from me; nevertheless, not My will, but Your will be done."

Jesus found Himself at a crossroads to which He appropriately responded, "Nevertheless, not My will, but Your will be done." Submitting to the Father's will is always the right response and at times, it is the hardest response. This account of Jesus in the garden gives a depiction of every believer who struggles with who they are and what they are called to do. To be. To effect change. It is the intersection of the Lord's plan for our lives and our view of the life we plan for ourselves. Ahh, yes. What a conflict!

The text loudly speaks of things from which we would much rather hide. We find it easier to keep our heads down and just survive the night. But we cannot. I cannot shrink back from my assignment! You cannot ignore the call on your life! The cost for our freedom - the collective freedom of the Body of Christ and every individual represented therein - was too great. The cost for our eternal salvation was being paid in this garden. This Gethsemane.

DAY ONE

Every person committed to interceding for others knows what it is like to press into prayer on the behalf of someone who is unwilling to do so for themselves. Who do you find yourself struggling to pray for in this season? Who are those close to you that you feel should be offering support as your go further into the garden? Take the time to align your heart with the heart of Jesus and begin to pray for them despite the difficulty.

DAY TWO

The spirit is willing, but the flesh is weak (Matthew 26:41). How often do we allow this to be an excuse to not obey God? This verse is Jesus acknowledging our weakness and inability to accomplish the hard things on our own.

When was the last time you allowed your flesh to keep you from praying for someone with whom you had a disagreement? What is God asking you to accept in order to surrender to His will in this area?

_____
_____
_____
_____
_____
_____
_____
_____
_____
_____
_____
_____
_____
_____
_____
_____
_____

DAY THREE

Consider the ways you can accept and embrace the Lord's will to live a life of faith that is pleasing to Him. In the space below, ask God to align your heart's desires with His plan for your life.

GO A LITTLE FURTHER...

What would it take to relinquish the idea of who you *think* you are to embrace who the Father wants you to be?

List the mindsets, habits, relationships, and anything else you believe needs to be released in order for you to become the God-ordained version of you. Describe in detail how your life would look if you were who the Father created you to be.

_____
_____
_____
_____
_____
_____
_____
_____
_____
_____
_____
_____
_____
_____
_____
_____
_____

THE GARDEN PRAYER
Week Four

Therefore we also, since we are surrounded by so great a cloud of witnesses, let us lay aside every weight, and the sin which so easily ensnares us, and let us run with endurance the race that is set before us, 2 looking unto Jesus, the author and finisher of our faith, who for the joy that was set before Him endured the cross, despising the shame, and has sat down at the right hand of the throne of God.

Hebrews 12:1-2

Thanks be to God who *always* leads us in triumph in Christ (2 Corinthians 2:14)! Jesus is writing our stories and - spoiler alert - WE WIN! Although our victory was secured on the Cross, we still have work to do. In addition to denying ourselves, picking up our crosses, and following Jesus, there are things we need to let go of. Weights like sin, negative thinking, distracting habits, and unfruitful relationships have to be shed. And, as we have been discussing for the last few weeks, garden seasons must be embraced. Champions are birthed through challenges, and victories are preceded by battles. No trials, no trophies. How we steward hard places matters.

The garden initiates a process that has critical checkpoints. Each point moves us closer to triumph. The checkpoints require our yes. Our faith in God. Our surrender to the Father's will. Let us continue examining Jesus' encounter with the Garden of Gethsemane to better understand how to navigate our hard places:

36 Then Jesus went with them to a place called Gethsemane, and he said to his disciples, "Sit here, while I go over there and pray." 37 And taking with him Peter and the two sons of Zebedee, he began to be sorrowful and troubled. 38 Then he said to them, "My soul is very sorrowful, even to death; remain here, and watch with me." 39 And going a little farther he fell on his face and prayed, saying, "My Father, if it be possible, let this cup pass from me; nevertheless, not as I will, but as you will." 40 And he came to the disciples and found them sleeping. And he said to Peter, "So, could you not watch with me one hour? 41 Watch and pray that you may not enter into temptation. The spirit indeed is willing, but the flesh is weak." 42 Again, for the second time, he went away and prayed, "My Father, if this cannot pass unless I drink it, your will be done." 43 And again he came and found them sleeping, for their eyes were heavy. 44 So, leaving them again, he went away and prayed for the third time, saying the same words again.

Matthew 26:36-44, ESV

THE MISSION

The Cross was no surprise to Jesus. He was completely aware of what He was sent to do. The terms of the mission were agreed upon long before wrapping Himself in flesh. David, Isaiah, Jeremiah, Joel, and other Old Testament prophets spoke of His coming. Jesus even told the disciples He would have to leave them! The redemption strategy was in place from the beginning. This is why Revelation 13:8 calls Him the Lamb slain from the foundation of the world. So, here we have it: Plan - Understood. Jesus - Willing.

When we find ourselves in extremely hard places, it is tempting to murmur, "Well, that's Jesus, not me?" We are no exception. God is the God of purpose. Everything He does - including creating us - is done with purpose in mind. We each have an assignment to complete.

8 For it is by grace you have been saved, through faith—and this is not from yourselves, it is the gift of God— 9 not by works, so that no one can boast. 10 For we are God's handiwork, created in Christ Jesus to do good works, which God prepared in advance for us to do.

Ephesians 2:8-10, NIV

THE SECRET PLACE

Let's revisit Matthew 26:36: *Then Jesus went with them to a place called Gethsemane, and he said to his disciples, "Sit here, while I go over there and pray."* Jesus left His companions and went a little further. He brought a few friends. This could have been for comfort or support. The text doesn't tell us the reason. My second point is this: There are some places in prayer that only require you and God.

There is not enough room in the hard place for everyone we would like to bring. Furthermore, not everyone is equipped to endure, press in, or make sacrifices the way that the garden requires. The solitude may feel isolating and a bit frustrating, but here is where your faith and resolve are purified.

1 He who dwells in the secret place of the Most High
Shall abide under the shadow of the Almighty.

2 I will say of the LORD, "He is my refuge and my fortress;
My God, in Him I will trust."

3 Surely He shall deliver you from the snare of the fowler
And from the perilous pestilence.

4 He shall cover you with His feathers,
And under His wings you shall take refuge;
His truth shall be your shield and buckler.

Psalm 91:1-4

THE QUESTIONS

Jesus goes off to pray, and although we hear what He prays, we never hear the Father's response. What is happening here? We have seen it recorded in Scripture where God responds. He talks to Abraham and Moses and the other prophets. God responded to Job even. So why not Jesus? Can you imagine the conversation? Jesus went back three times, asking if there was any chance the cup could pass Him by. For what? He wanted a workaround. Is there another way? Can we change the plan? And we do the same thing. While in prayer.

What do you think the Father said to Jesus? His will had already been communicated. Whatever He spoke was enough to keep Jesus committed to the cause. What has God spoken to you? You know your mission. All that is left is obediently going further into the garden.

12 Therefore, my beloved, as you have always obeyed, so now, not only as in my presence but much more in my absence, work out your own

salvation with fear and trembling, 13 for it is God who works in you, both to will and to work for his good pleasure.

Philippians 2:12-13, ESV

THE FIGHT

Is it easier to see yourself in the garden now? We all end up here at some point, going around the same mountain in our lives because we absolutely do not want to yield to the will of the Father. Us. You. Me. We go into prayer and stay for a while. Sometimes our motive for prayer is just to satisfy the requirement, and we walk away believing our responsibility is actually over. Ha! We hope to reconcile our conscience with our duty and be able to say, "Well, I prayed about it. It's in God's hands now."

How many times do we walk away from prayer, leaving the garden to return to our friends and life as usual, and nothing has changed? I am not talking about our circumstances not changing - those definitely haven't changed! I am referring to the burdens that remain, the fears that still have a stronghold on us and others, addictions, illnesses, and lack. There is no peace or joy, but we feel as though we did our due diligence. How???

Prayer is tied to purpose. Our life's purpose. A purpose that changes the world! Jesus said that greater works than He did, we can do (John 14:2). These works are tied to people - ordinary people like you and me - who are purposed to perform them. Look around. Hopelessness and bondage stretch as far as the eyes can see. People, we have work to do.

DAY ONE

What Mission is the Father calling you to fulfill in this hard place, and what are you willing to endure to remain close to during this garden experience?

_____

DAY TWO

Ephesians 2:10 tells us we are created for great works. What do you believe you are purposed to do? Remember that the measurement for greatness is in the eyes of God. It does not matter if the world calls your calling small or insignificant. If you are unsure, ask the Father what He wants to do in and through your life. You are created for great works! Begin today achieving what God has called you to do.

DAY THREE

Perhaps you are willing to live for God and work out His purpose for your life but struggle to know for sure what that is. Ask God where He wants you to start. Don't be afraid. The Lord *wants* you to serve Him, and He will definitely show you the work He wants you to do.

GO A LITTLE FURTHER...

The beauty of the garden is that it has a way of revealing the deeper layers of our purpose while also exposing the thorns of our humanity.

What beauty is the Father revealing to you during our journey together? What facets of your humanity do you find yourself fighting to subdue?

_____
_____
_____
_____
_____
_____
_____
_____
_____
_____
_____
_____
_____
_____
_____
_____
_____
_____

THE PLACE OF ACCEPTANCE
Week Five

44 So He left them, went away again, and prayed the third time, saying the same words. 45 Then He came to His disciples and said to them, "Are you still sleeping and resting? Behold, the hour is at hand, and the Son of Man is being betrayed into the hands of sinners. 46 Rise, let us be going. See, My betrayer is at hand."

Matthew 26:44-46

The hour is at hand. Wait. Now?! What happened between Jesus' third time going away to pray and His returning to the disciples? What took place is crystal clear. Jesus didn't just pray to fulfill a requirement; He prayed until He was able to accept the will of God for His life.

It is simple and yet, so profound. The answer is prayer. Every time. ALWAYS. The Father's will is what we must lean into all the more when we find ourselves in the garden... and we all eventually end up in the garden. How can I be so sure? Because God has a way of calling us to hard places. That is the reality of the believer. Before Jesus ever performed a miracle, He was led by the Spirit into the wilderness for a forty-day fast that ended with being tempted by Satan (Matthew 4:1-11). It happens. This is a part of the trying of our faith that must take place.

Some works we are called to for the advancement of the Kingdom require a deeper degree of surrender. To get to this next level, we must go a little further into the garden of prayer. Naturally speaking, a garden is not just some random piece of ground. It is a plot of land set aside for a particular purpose. It has soil that must be constantly tended to. Sown into and then worked in. You don't just visit a garden; you work in it.

Our Lord gave us a beautiful example of this part of our relationship with God. He modeled how it should look and feel. Things grow in gardens. Fruit and vegetables - things we can consume for our nourishment - come from this particular place. This purposeful place. And yet, we treat the place of prayer like a farmers market - where we can go to purchase the fruit of someone else's labor in prayer.

In this hard place - in this garden - Jesus showed us how to live the good life. It is a life of peace, love, and joy in the Holy Spirit that comes only by doing the will of God. And yes, the good life includes gardens. How does that relate to everything we have discussed so far? How does this help anyone? I am glad you asked because there is another question that must first be answered.

What does further look like?

We know there are different reasons for prayer and more than one kind of prayer. However, the focus here is not to get revelation on a matter or receive an answer or even to make a request for something to be given. How many of us already know what God wants us to do with our lives? With our money? With our gifts? With our time? We often know what is expected of us. We simply choose to forge our own path, to do things our way. Is it that we don't *want* to submit or are *afraid* to submit?

Getting what He needed from the Father brought Jesus to a place of acceptance. He got up, went back to His friends, and said, "Arise, let us be going." During the chapters that follow, the world watched as this God made of flesh was betrayed by someone He called "friend." He was then tried in a people's court of His enemies, wrongfully convicted, beaten, and nailed to a cross. He was persecuted, spat on, mocked, and publicly rejected. Through it all, we don't see any other record of an earlier depressed state as read back in verse 38. In fact, intercession for the accusers had already begun. Jesus asked the Father to forgive His persecutors for they did not know what they were doing.

What Jesus received in that garden conversation was the answer He needed to fulfill His purpose. I imagine the answer was something along the lines of, "Because it pleases Me." And because it pleased His father, Jesus became the ultimate sacrifice. Just like that.

How many of us are avoiding the garden conversation, where we really ask God how to resolve a situation or a plan for receiving our healing? We ask, but do we sit still and silent long enough to get an answer?

Jesus did not leave the garden empty handed. Because of the garden conversation with His Father, He received:

- Acceptance - He made the decision and agreed to all it entailed to purchase our freedom from the penalty of sin.
- Strength - He was strengthened to bear the Cross, including all the pain and rejection that came with it.

- Peace - He knew the Father would be completely pleased with His obedience, and that gave Him the peace needed to endure the hard place.

Are you still unsure about how to go a little further? The perfect start is by showing up in the world as the light you were created to be. You are destined to push back against the darkness. You are called to effect change in the world. Go a little further into the garden. The garden is truly for your good.

14 "You are the light of the world. A city set on a hill cannot be hidden. 15 Nor do people light a lamp and put it under a basket, but on a stand, and it gives light to all in the house. 16 In the same way, let your light shine before others, so that they may see your good works and give glory to your Father who is in heaven.

Matthew 5:14-16

Those nevertheless moments are not easy, but they are crucial to a successful Christian walk. Is your heart's cry, "Father, I just want to please you?" If so, what are you willing to do for His good pleasure? Waht are you willing to forsake, turn away from, or accept? Oftentimes, stepping into the will of God for our lives is a simple matter of acceptance. Are you willing to be led into the garden, as Jesus was led into the wilderness? Are you willing to be led into a place of sacrifice and submission in prayer?

DAY ONE

There is purpose in the garden. Lean in the garden. Lean into the voice of the Father as you answer the following questions:

What gifts and talents do I possess that I am afraid of using for God and why?

_____
_____
_____
_____
_____
_____
_____
_____
_____
_____
_____
_____
_____
_____
_____
_____
_____
_____
_____
_____
_____
_____
_____
_____
_____

What will be my motivation for moving forward in the purpose and calling God has for my life?

DAY TWO

Identify the situations and spaces that cause your light to shine the brightest.

How can you make the conscious decision to glorify God with your life?

What would it look like to simply shine and accept what comes along with obedience, trusting God to use it for your good?

DAY THREE

The Father is with you in the garden. He is showing you the way. How will you begin living on another level of faithful obedience today?

_____
_____
_____
_____
_____
_____
_____
_____
_____
_____
_____
_____
_____
_____
_____
_____
_____
_____
_____
_____
_____
_____
_____

Describe in detail what the next level of faith looks like for you.

GO A LITTLE FURTHER...

Reflect on the last 5 weeks of your garden experience. How have you grown? What revelation have you received?

_____
_____
_____
_____
_____
_____
_____
_____
_____
_____
_____
_____
_____
_____
_____
_____
_____
_____
_____
_____
_____
_____
_____
_____
_____

How has your view of the Garden of Gethsemane shifted?

UNIL NEXT TIME
A Prayer for You

Now, if you are ready - only if you truly ready, recite this prayer in spirit and in truth:

Father,

    I pray that Your will is made clear and manifested in my life. Give me the courage needed to pick up my assignment, take up my cross, and wholeheartedly follow closely after You.

    You are the author and finisher of my faith, and I believe You are able to keep me from falling as I follow after You. Thank You, Father, for providing this garden experience where I can bring my hurts, doubts and fears and, in turn, receive direction and strength for the journey ahead.

    My prayer is that Your kingdom will come for me and that Your will be done in me as I seek to walk out Your desire and perfect plan for my life. In the name of Jesus I pray. Amen.

ABOUT THE AUTHOR

Sandra Bitten understands the mandate on her life and fully embraces the call to develop God's people for triumphant lives of purpose. With revelatory wisdom and an even tone, she challenges believers to hold fast to the Lord's precepts, trust in His faithfulness, and courageously walk in destiny no matter what life brings their way. As an intercessor, teacher, and minister of the Gospel for thirty years, Sandra remains fully persuaded that we are ordained to effect change in the earth.

Sandra Bitten is a native of Huntsville, Alabama who now calls the Greater Nashville area "home." She is the proud mother of one musically gifted son, Kris, and mother-in-love to his psalmist wife, Shataria. Sandra is an IPEC certified Life Purpose and Executive Coach and is currently enrolled in Regent University's Masters in Pastoral Counseling program. Sandra's aim is to continue equipping pastors and ministry leaders to serve God and the world by serving their core values.

Made in the USA
Columbia, SC
07 July 2024